FUN Wheeled American Style

MANDY RUZICKA

authorHOUSE®

AuthorHouse™
1663 Liberty Drive
Bloomington, IN 47403
www.authorhouse.com
Phone: 1 (800) 839-8640

Published by AuthorHouse 01/18/2016

ISBN: 978-1-5049-7217-8 (sc)
ISBN: 978-1-5049-7216-1 (e)

Acknowledgements

First of all thank you to God for giving me a second chance at life after my accident.

Thank you to everyone who told me no and put me down, you made me stronger!

Thank you to my sister Angela (insert inside joke here) for being the best big sister ever and for always supporting me and giving me an over whelming amount of encouragement and love and for just inspiring me in general. I love you.

Thank you to my mom and dad for not giving up on me and for teaching me I can do whatever I want if I put my mind to it… even if it is short lived. Especially my dad for the encouragement and positive attitude and kind words.

To my teacher Dr. Klund, thank you for putting up with me for 4 years. Ha ha, I wrote more than a sentence! And thanks to my editors, mom and Brenda, who changed just enough to make my story readable.

The goal of this book is to show that people in wheelchairs really can have a lot of fun. And that we too live "normal" lives. After all there shouldn't be an ability level on fun, right?!

What is fun? Noun: Enjoyment, amusement, or lighthearted pleasure: "Anyone who turns up can join in the fun." Adjective: Amusing, entertaining, or enjoyable: "It was a fun evening." Verb: Joke or tease: "No need to get sore- I was only funning"; "They are just funning you." Synonyms: Amusement, joke, sport, jest, or lark.

Who can argue with that?! Hi, my name is Mandy, I was born with Spina Bifida (Latin for split spine) a.k.a. "The Wheeled American." How cool of a super hero name would that be?! Anyway, I'd like to start by talking about what I consider fun. These are just my views and opinions, making this officially "unauthorized" by anyone but me.

Chapter 1

Rock wall climbing with DASA (Disabled Athlete Sports Association)

How can someone in a chair climb a rock wall you ask? Here's how, first I got strapped into a harness while I was still sitting in my wheelchair. Then to get started I got lifted up in the seated position by a rope and pulley type thing and then got picked up and put on the wall (kind of like a fly). For a 170 pound person that can't use her feet or legs it's not the best feeling in the world. While on the wall I was instructed to climb to the nearest rocks I saw and pull myself up to the next and yada, yada, yada. I felt great but kind of scared at the same time. The whole time I heard "Great job Mandy you can do it!" "There's the next rock, see it?" from my friends and the coach. Do you remember the part in Finding Nemo when Dory was singing "just keep swimming just keep swimming, swimming, swimming" well I was doing that in my head but saying the word climbing. All the sudden I looked up and I said "Oh my gosh, that's high!" Yay! I made it to the top! I was exhausted by the time I came down. I waited a while, had lunch and did it all again. It felt wonderful!

"*There is no greater disability in society, than the inability to see a person as more.*"

Robert M. Hensel

Chapter 2

Angela and I

The most fun I have is with my sister, Angela. We have been through so much together over the years. She's my best friend! I can recall one time just recently we went to read her "Wendy on Wheels" books to the campers at the MDA camp in Fredricktown, Mo. She is an author. What

a blast! Wendy on Wheels is about a ten year old girl who uses a wheelchair and goes on all kinds of fun adventures and faces some obstacles that she tries to fix and has a few things to say about them, and causes a little mischief, along the way. On the way there and back we saw all these cute statues of pink elephants and a cow. We were driving home and she said "You know what Mooch, that's my nickname, I would really like to get my picture taken with that pink elephant one day." I looked at her and said "So would I, let's do it!" She said, "This has been on my bucket list for a while." Why a thirty two year old has a bucket list, I'll never know but regardless, her husband Andrew would never do it. So we found a car dealership with an elephant statue and a big cow statue too. We got out of the car and went to take a picture of us with it. Angela said "I'd like to be in the picture too. I wonder if someone inside will take our picture with it?" With that Angela went inside. A few minutes later she came out with a really sweet lady that took our picture. We thanked her and the lady told us about the inside of the building. She said "Come inside we have a lot of cool things to take pictures of." Omg, it was like a museum! We found some really cool things! I looked at her excitedly and said "This is the best day of my adult life!"

Technically this one is gray with pinks spots, but you get the point. This was at a car dealership along the way home.

Chapter 3

SBYA Cruise and Conference

I also had the chance to go on the SBYA (Spina Bifida young adult) cruise. That was amazing! I met so many really awesome people around my age. I also got to experience so many things on and off the ship. On the ship they had a lot of shows, karaoke, food, drinks and like a thousand, I'm exaggerating but a lot pools and a casino. My favorite part was dinner in the dining room. Off the ship we went to the Cayman Islands, Haiti, and Jamaica. In the Cayman Islands we went to a place called Hell, a turtle farm - my favorite part of the whole trip, and the rum cake factory. In Jamaica we went shopping which wasn't too exciting, and the people were annoying! Haiti was really fun. We went to Nelly's Beach which was a private beach that only the SBYA could use. My dad didn't like that too much because he was busy pushing not only my chair but other people's chairs through the sand. Other than that it was beautiful!

I was also fortunate enough to go to the national Spina Bifida conference. That was fun, too. My favorite part is the adult day trips to somewhere like a ball game or something. And the nights at the bars with my friends!!! Let me tells you, a whole room full of people in wheelchairs is so much fun and kinda crazy at the same time. Especially after some of us have been drinking! I love my friends and I don't know what I'd do without them!! I also enjoy the days with the vendors. It's cool to see all the wheelchairs and supplies and equipment for sale. Angela also wrote a book for a catheter company called 180 Medical. It is all about teaching little ones how to self-cath and that it's ok to use a catheter. That was being given away at the 180 booth. I also enjoyed meeting my sister's friends. I love that we all have things in common also. We are all so close it feels like a family.

Chapter 4

Variety and the White House

I belonged to an organization when I was little called St. Louis Variety the Children's Charity. They buy medical equipment and provide a positive and fun environment for children with physical and mental disabilities in and around the St. Louis area. I was their poster child when I was two years old. They have helped me tremendously!! I have been a camp counselor for them, I was involved in the choir, volunteered in the office, and much more. Now they have all become my family as well! I was involved in the choir since they started it when I was a freshman in high school all the way up to a senior in high school. The most fun was we all flew to Washington, DC to sing at the White House. It was very exciting! I was also very nervous because I had a solo. I was hoping the president would have been there. That's when Bush 43 was in office…I won't open up that can of worms! We got to sing for the people visiting and his cute little Scottie dog. I loved it. I would have thought the security would have been better though.

This is me with my Dad at my first Telethon.
I was pretty cute, wasn't I?

Chapter 5

Concerts and Famous people

I have also been fortunate to experience a number of things including going to see Donny Osmond, Backstreet boys and Glee live in concert. Those things were all fun! I also got to meet some amazing people both on my own and with Variety. I've gotten met most of the Rams, Sammy Davis Jr., Lou Rawls, The Dallas Cowboy cheerleaders, and the list goes on. But the person I was most impressed with meeting is one of my favorite actors, author, musician, and director Mr. Chris Colfer. I got to meet him twice. He's very nice! And his books are amazing! They are called The Land of Stories. First series I have willingly read since high school. We have been to Indianapolis and Chicago to see him. I even gave him a gift that he thanked me for after the Glee Live show. Awesome night!! We also got to see him at the St. Louis library where he had 2 book signing and Q&A sessions for his latest Land of Stories books. So that's now four times I've gotten to see him, holy cow! I was so nervous! He's my favorite person ever!!! I love him.

This is Chris Colfer, me, my grandma, and Steve Chris's body guard at Chris's first Land of Stories book signing.

Chapter 6

Swimming with Dolphins and the Beach Wheelchair

I have been on many fun vacations. The ones that stick out the most are going to Sea World in Orlando, Florida. We got to swim with dolphins. It was so fun. I also got to swim in the ocean in Clearwater, Florida. My parents rented a beach wheelchair so I could swim. I had not done that before. At first it was kind of scary. My dad pushed me into the water and the waves were splashing all around me. One even knocked me out of the chair. The water was really cold. I also swam in the water without the chair for a while. That was my first time using a beach wheelchair and even though it was tough pushing all over the beach in the sand, I thought it was well worth it and I am very glad I got the chance to experience it!

Me and dad on the beach in Florida. This is the vacation that inspired the Wendy on Wheels books.

Chapter 7

Races for Charities and Volunteering

I have also done a variety of 5ks and "runs" for local charities. I do these with my mom and my sister and friend. I love doing these because it gives me plenty of exercise, it's fun and for a good cause. In our most recent race, we did a heart walk for my mom's friend's daughter whose daughter has a heart defect from birth. Although I got pushed most of the way it was still a lot of fun. I also volunteered for a dog and puppy rescue called Flaw Dogs. I loved it! I was always asked to hold the dogs and puppies that had "flaws". They were mostly the ones that weren't socialized or scared of people. Who wouldn't want to spend their Saturdays holding adorable puppies?! I always tried to get them adopted and put in good words for them with their soon to be new owners. Sadly, Flaw Dogs has disbanded due to the health and age of the owner and volunteers. Now I do the same for our own Vet's pet rescue.

Ang, me and Mom at the Heart Walk.

Yes, this is a Llama. Dr. Doug helps take care of all animals.

Chapter 8

Embroidery Corner

I so love to do embroidery! I learned from my mom. I also put together a store I created on Facebook. I sell some of the things I make to whoever sees and likes my work. I put together a price list, business cards and a book of things that I have made but mostly give things away to my family and friends. I love doing it and I hope to make an actual business of it one day. Every time I finish a pillowcase, baby bib or guest towel I feel like I like I have really accomplished something and I am proud of my work. I started selling things to pay for the national Spina Bifida conferences and cruises.

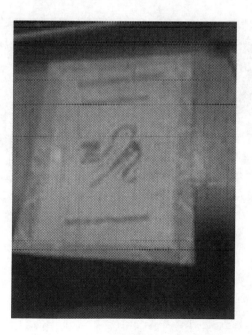

This is the business card I made for Embroidery Corner.

Chapter 9

Crocheting Baby Blankets, Scarves, and Shawls

I really love to crochet. I was taught by my grandmother, Grandma Lu, who also crochets. Did I mention, I love crocheting?! I have made many things for people. I enjoy making baby afghans the most. I make them for my family and friends with new babies. I have a lot of yarn and make them in a variety of colors and types of yarn. It is fun to go shopping with my grandma to buy crochet hooks and yarn. I love doing it downstairs in my dad's "man land" where there's a TV but mostly grandma and I work at the kitchen table. We get to talk and visit while doing something worthwhile.

A blanket I was working on for my cousin.

Chapter 10

Dancing on the Telethon

When I was about seven or eight I used to dance with a dance company called A Very Special Arts. It was one of the organizations supported by Variety. Every week I used to go to Studio C where the classes were held. My teacher's name was Judy Arkus, her daughter owned Studio C. I was the only person in the class so I got Judy all to myself. I was the only person in a wheelchair she had ever worked with. She was a nurse and practiced my routines in a wheelchair at work. I also got to make up my own routines and perform them for Judy. I loved it!! Variety let me dance on their telethon back when was there was one. I would also dance in competitions. One time I got the opportunity to dance in a competition in Brussels, Belgium. We chose not to go because I don't travel well and it cost too much. After a few years, I decided not to do it anymore because we moved and I lost interest. I wish I had decided to stick with it! I loved to dress up in the beautiful costumes and wear makeup. I thought it was a very cool thing to get to wear makeup. I really loved performing!

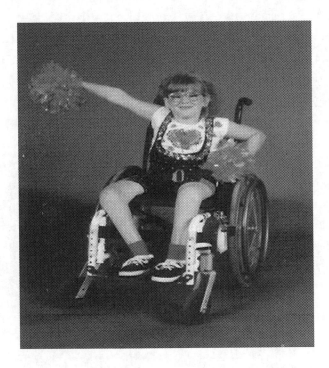

Me dancing on the telethon when I was around
ten. My teacher made my outfit for me.

Chapter 11

Working out at Paraquad

Now I belong to an organization called Paraquad. They are a non-profit organization that helps people with disabilities reach their full potential in the community and in life. I am involved in their health and wellness program. It consists of a fully accessible gym for people with disabilities. They have all kinds of equipment that I can use in my wheelchair. They have trainers, physical therapy students and a chiropractor too. I have two trainers that I really like that encourage and help me to do my very best. They work me out so hard!! It's a 12 week program and I'm on my sixth week having already lost 8 lbs. I feel it is very important to keep your whole body and your mind fit. I really appreciate that Paraquad has a place to work out for me and individuals like me. Independence is very important to me and Paraquad gives me that and a sense that I can accomplish things on my own! I have met some very nice people who participate in the program and my trainer is awesome, too. One time she called me a "bad ass" and I liked it.

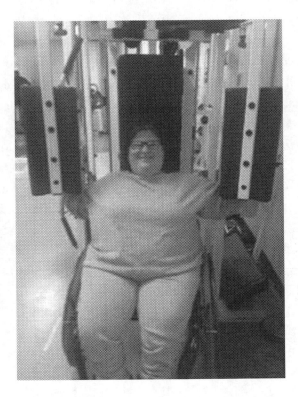

This is me working out on the butterfly press.

Chapter 12

Official Wendy business

What I think is the most fun of all is going with my sister to share the Wendy on Wheels message. I love helping her spread the word about inclusion and equality. We speak at schools and summer camps, reading a portion of the book and encouraging the children to talk about their feelings. They ask lots of questions and are generally interested in learning more about Wendy. They also ask me and my sister questions about our lives, if we always get along and things like that. They are so adorable and smart. I'm really glad I get to be part of such a powerful and meaningful project. It's very important for me to be an advocate for myself and other people with disabilities.

I am always looking for new things to do and may get the opportunity to speak to students through college abilities awareness days. I really enjoy doing something that I feel so passionately about and that's much bigger then myself. I hope to do a lot more speaking with SLU at programs that are offered throughout the community. What I didn't realize is, there are classes devoted to disability empowerment and advocacy. I love the idea that there are whole departments devoted to disabilities and raising awareness.

I really hope to do this for a career. I think it's very important for everyone to know that we are just people who do things in different ways. I really identify with Angela's fourth book in the series "Wendy on Wheels Takes a Stand". The story is about bullying and how to stand up to bullies. I have been bullied a lot in my life and it's really empowering to teach positive ways to deal with bullies. When I was younger, I didn't know how to do that. It's almost therapeutic for me to talk about my experiences now and share my coping stories with everyone. I was taught to treat people how I would want to be treated. It makes me feel good to help others. Children are the key to the future and we can teach them at a young age to include everyone and treat them with respect.

Chapter 13

Work can be Fun

I've had a few jobs I thought were fun. I started working in the summer of my sophomore year, at latch key programs and summer schools. I loved to see and hang out with all the kids. I got paid $6.50 an hour. It was good for me to learn work skills, get up early, have a schedule and look nice every day.

I also worked at Jack in the Box when I was in my twenties. It was fun in the beginning. I did everything from food prep to run the register to cleaning tables and greeting guests. I met a lot of nice people. It was an experience I'll never forget. I worked four hours a day, from 10-2, every day which got old.

I prefer the work programs with the children though. I would like to work in a classroom with kids that have disabilities. I have a cousin that had very severe cerebral palsy. I loved my cousin but he died due to complications from his disability. Another great job was working at Variety's Summer Camp for children who are differently abled or disadvantaged. There motto was "I Can!" We did all kinds of activities with the kids and went on field trips. I got paid for having fun, awesome. Those kids totally amazed and inspired me every day. They didn't let anything get in the way of what they wanted to do or get them down. Plus, they were all very sweet. I was also involved in a Sports Camp for special kids one summer, I was in charge of arts and crafts. I really loved that too!

I recently started volunteering for the St. Vincent de Paul society thrift shop near my house. I love it! I work in the clothes department hanging shirts. I work part time, a few days a week. They recently moved to a new location. I meet a lot of really nice people. There are about 6 other people in my department that put the shirts out on the floor after I put them on hangers. It is a great experience for me. I like to get out of the house a little bit too. I might see about doing it full time as a paying job. That's how much I like it. I definitely see myself staying there for a while. Every once in a while my family comes in to see me and look around. My mom even came in to help with a few friends on my birthday. I think it is cool that Wendy volunteered too.

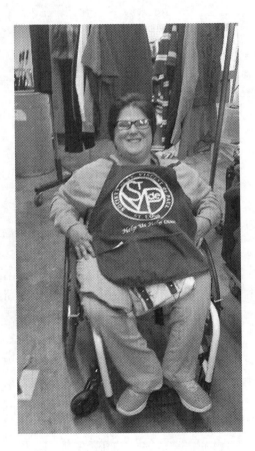

Chapter 14

Special gymnastics and Sports and Gym Class

The one thing I loved in school was gym class. I loved my physical therapists and being a part of the class. It made me feel normal for an hour a day. I loved all the activities we did.

The thing I liked the most is every year they had a gymnastics assembly. I loved being a part of that. I would do floor exercises and climb the cargo net. I also played tennis with the St. Louis Wheelchair Sports Association. We would play outside and it was very hot because it was summer, on an asphalt court. I met some friends there and played with my boyfriend at the time, who was quite good. I had a blast even though I was terrible!

I also loved to lift weights in high school. It made me feel really strong and powerful. And let me tell you, I could lift a lot of weight. There were mostly guys in the class. Sometimes, we got to roller skate. I loved rolling around in a huge circle with my chair to Lauren Hill's song "That Thing." The room lights were really low in the gym with all kinds of fun colors. It looked just like a roller rink.

Chapter 15

Variety Children's Theater and the Muny

Variety has a program called Variety Children's Theater. They put on professional plays in the auditorium of a local university. I have seen "The Wizard of OZ" and "Oliver." I look forward to it every year. The plays are always in October and a lot of my friends are actors and actresses. It is so much fun to see individuals with varying abilities participating together, professional actors and amateurs, disabled and able bodied actors. The shows are always very good.

I also love going to the Muny and seeing shows each summer. Professional and local actors and actresses put on stage plays and musicals. The stage is outside in a huge park with lots of big trees. We bring food and sit at picnic tables to eat in the park before the show. It's always my favorite part of the summer! We try to pick a night that is not too hot. This year the weather was beautiful. They have special seating for wheelchairs, a concession stand and really cool programs that tell you how many acts there are and about all the actresses, actors and crew. I love musicals. I think my favorite one to see is "Wicked." I also love to get all dressed up. It makes me feel good!

Chapter 16

Super Heroes

I love Superman!! I really liked Christopher Reeve also. After his accident I was truly inspired by his determination to walk again and I respected him for that. He did a lot of great things. In addition to raising awareness and money for spinal cord injury research, he had his own foundation.

The other night I went to a presentation about super heroes that have disabilities. That is what makes them super heroes. A professor who taught a disability class at Washington University gave the talk. It was very interesting and I loved it! I felt very special after it was over. He showed super heroes with prosthetics, Spina bifida, intellectual disabilities and some that were blind.

There was a table that had containers full of marbles with signs on them that said put a marble in if you know someone with a physical disability, put one in if you know someone that's blind and on and on. I came to the one that said put one in if you know someone that has a physical disability and I asked if I could put the whole stack in since I know a lot of people with disabilities. Angela and I talked to the speaker after he was done speaking. Angela showed him her Wendy books and I showed him my tattoo. Yes, I have a Superman tattoo.

The college campus is gigantic all spread out. It took a while for us to get from the parking lot to the room where it was being held. My feet kept falling off my foot rests and getting caught underneath them which made it harder for me to move. It felt like it took forever to get to the van. I was very tired on the way home but so glad I went. It made me feel good to hear others talk about people with disabilities as super heroes and know what I accomplished with my super powers.

Chapter 17

The Wheeled American card

I love the fact I get to go to the head of lines at Six Flags or at concerts. One time at the Greek festival I just rolled to the front of the food line and nobody said anything or cared. I also butt in the line when we saw Chris Colfer this last time. It was nice because it was really hot. Nobody said anything that time either. I got out of the van in the middle of the line and someone said do you need to get through? I said, "Yes, I do" and rolled my way through. I always say I pulled the Wheeled American card again. Not everyone likes it but it's one of the many perks of being in a wheelchair.

I also get to sit in the front row at concerts. When I went to my friend Alisse's dance recital with my mom, we went to the very front row. My mom's friend said, "How did you get front row seats?" My mom said, "Because I'm with the Mooch." He said, "Oh that's not fair, she's like a criminal" and I laughed. I knew he was just kidding.

I remember going to Six Flags with my family and getting to sit in the front of the line to get on the water rides. It really annoyed people! I also got to stay on and ride each ride twice. It was the same for all the shows. I would get a special section for my chair. I also got to do things that other people wouldn't get to do, like wait for the singers in a special spot outside of the Fox theatre.

I like to think I get special treatment because I have a disability which probably isn't true. That also sometimes annoys people. I like it though because it makes me feel special. I also love getting all dressed up which gives people more of a reason to stare at me. I usually look very pretty with make up on and everything. The first time I met Donny Osmond I even got my ears pierced.

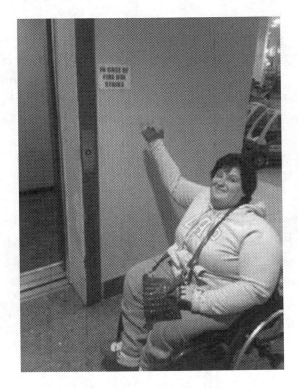

Uh, not so much!

Chapter 18

Surgeries and Recovery Time

I have had a lot of surgeries in my life. Back surgery, bladder surgery, eyes, shunt, and my legs. But the most fun part is the recovery time especially when I was in school and I got to miss. I got to watch TV all day and eat whatever I wanted.

One time there was a six month recovery period. I had a lot of visitors and got presents. I also had some teachers that would come to the house while I recovered, well that part kind of sucked though. I loved when my extended family would stay with me while my parents worked. We played video games…a lot of video games. I actually liked some of the hospital stays. I got whatever I wanted and I didn't have to ask. I ate all kind of food and treats, and played in the play room. I made friends with some of the patients, doctors, and nurses.

I also have a lot of fun with my dad when he is recovering from surgeries. I get to do the same things I mentioned while taking care of my best friend. He has had a lot of surgeries too over the last couple of years. It makes me feel really good to be his nurse. I love to feel useful and help people. I guess surgeries can be fun and it's true that what doesn't kill us makes us stronger.

My surgery survival songs are "Fighter" by Christina Aguilera and "Survivor" by Destiny's Child. My most recent surgery was rough though. I was in a lot of pain and I felt like I'd never get better. It felt like I was out of commission for a long time. I was kind of mad that we had to travel five hours away from home and I was in the hospital less than a week. I was supposed to be in the hospital for 2 to 3 weeks. I felt rushed by the people taking care of me. They didn't allow me to feel the pain after the surgery. I was on morphine and other drugs. I really didn't get a chance to feel anything so I never knew if I was really in pain or not, until I got home. The doctor's assistant took off the bandages and tape the day after the surgery.

I don't think I will be so polite and cooperative next time because I don't think that did me any good. I need to have the surgery again in the Fall, for the third time. Third times a charm I guess. The only part I did like was watching Glee with my friend and my mom. I got so excited when I saw Chris and heard him sing. It really snapped me out of it. It also meant the world to me that I got to see him after my recovery period had ended. That and meeting my new niece, baby Sally, were the best parts of that whole year.

Me, in a full body cast, after having rods put in my spine.

Chapter 19

What is Spina Bifida

Something else I consider fun is learning things I didn't know about my disability. Like, did you know that Spina Bifida is a birth defect? That's what I was born with and has lead me to my wheelchair. Spina bifida is also called split spine. It comes from a Latin word meaning split spine.

Every 1 in 10 babies are born with Spina Bifida, that's 2000 cases a year. Spina Bifida happens when a baby's spine isn't all the way formed properly in the womb which causes an open lesion on the back. It has to be surgically closed then forms a hump. It's not fully connected to the brain either which causes fluid on the brain. A shunt is then inserted to remove some of the excess fluid. The shunt causes many mental disabilities as well. Difficulties in math and comprehension sometimes even motor skills.

There are 3 main types of Spina Bifida. Spina Bifida Occulta which is the worst form and more rare, sometimes fatal. Meningocele and Myelomeningocele. That is the form I have. There many different levels and severities depending on where the split is located. It is caused by a lack of folic acid intake by the mother. Spina Bifida is usually followed by hydrocephalus. A symptom is an allergy to latex. It also causes bladder and bowel incontinence. In my own case, I can't drink things with a lot of caffeine.

Chapter 20

Yahtzee, Yahtzee and more Yahtzee

What is more fun than playing games? Yahtzee is my favorite game of all time! I play with my mom. We play at least 3 games a night. Sometimes she beats me and sometimes I beat her. We mostly play when she gets home from work some nights. Not only is it a lot of fun but I get to see her and spend time with her which I love. I think she enjoys it too. We have the best conversations while playing.

I wish my dad would play but he doesn't like to play games. We play after dinner. It's the best part of my long boring days. She gets very excited when she gets a yahtzee! She yells Ahh ha ha Yahtzee YES! Sometimes, I do it too. I get really mad when she says she's too tired to play, just because I enjoy it so much. I am not really too good at the adding part so my mom does it. The most points I have ever gotten was around 400 points but that's because I got four yahtzees in one game. Yahtzee keeps your mind sharp that's another reason I like to play. It makes me think. Sometimes I play by myself, if I accidentally leave the game out but that's not as much fun.

Chapter 21

Goofing Around

I love to be goofy and sing and dance around my house. I especially love to sing! I'm always singing! I love singing to Glee music the most. I pretend I'm Artie when "Don't stop Believin" is on. Sometimes my parents catch me doing it. I love taking my hair brush and singing into it. I also make up my own words. Sometimes I make funny sounds too…in private.

Sometime I goof around with my sister. We go on little car trips and turn the music up and sing at the top of our lungs. I laugh at the silliest things. Well, Ang and I both do that. I love to laugh and I love making other people laugh too. Sometimes I say things that some people think is funny and I don't mean it to be. Most of the times things come out wrong. I also make up my own songs sometimes. I just love to be happy in general.

Chapter 22

School Dances

I went to a ton of school dances in high school. I loved Homecoming and Prom. I also loved going to the homecoming football games. I went to my senior prom with my really good friend named Kevin. He is in a wheelchair, also. I loved getting my hair and nails done to get ready for it. I wanted to get an updo. I had a very pretty and long blue dress with glitter on it. It was held at the Millennium Center, which was decorated very pretty in the room. My cousins dressed as chauffers and drove us to the prom. Keven looked very handsome. He had a black tux on. A lot of my teachers were there to chaperone.

They had great food. The music was really great too. The room was huge. And all my friends where there. Kevin and I danced and took pictures. We also had some professional pictures taken too. My mom and his mom were going picture nuts. It think they enjoyed it just as much as we did. I also loved seeing my friends all dressed up in their beautiful dresses and suits. It was a fantastic night I'll never forget.

Chapter 23

My Sister's Wedding

I loved being in my sister's wedding. I was her maid of honor. The ceremony was beautiful. And, I love her husband, Andrew. The most fun part though I think was when we went to go get our hair and nails done with the wedding party. I had a very pretty dress and a flower crown. My cousins and my sister's friend were also bridesmaids. My little cousin, Illianna, was the flower girl. She looked so cute! Everyone looked beautiful and Andrew's bothers were the best men. We went to the wedding and to take pictures in a limo. That was fun! We had food and drinks in the limo.

The whole experience was so much fun. The limo had steps to get into it so I had to be lifted in my chair in to the limo. It was very high off the ground. And I was really scared. I thought I was going to get dropped. My dad lifted me the first time so I wasn't scared. Then Andrew made sure he was there to lift me. The food at dinner was great! And I even made a speech. That was scary. The dinner the night before the wedding was good too. Ang even gave me a gift. It was very fun. We went all around down town St. Louis for the pictures. It was a lot of up and down and in and out of the limo. It was a great night and awesome experience. I am so glad I was part of it!

Me and my parents with the newlyweds.

Chapter 24

Graduating from Parkway West

I also thought graduation was fun. I graduated from Parkway West High School in 2003. The ceremony was at Queeny Park in Chesterfield Mo. The ceremony was really long. I really enjoyed wearing the cap and gown. All my family and friends were there to congratulate me.

My grandparents came too. It was a beautiful day. It felt great rolling across that stage to get my diploma. My class was pretty big. I also thought the time before graduation was a little stressful too.

A lot happened in my senior year. I thought I almost wouldn't graduate. I hated finals week. Even though we got out of school early after them. I think my favorite class was my cooking class and that final was pretty easy.

I always loved graduation parties in the summer. I got invited to a lot of them and I had mine at my uncle's lake house in Desoto Mo when he still had it. I think the most fun party was my friend Kevin's. If I remember correctly it was at Pasta House. Both parties were a lot of fun!

Chapter 25

The Fabulous Fox Theater

I have seen many things at the Fox but I think my favorite show was when we got to see Straight No Chaser, or "Straight." They are my favorite acapella group. I went with my parents and my friend Emma. We didn't have handicapped seats so I had to sit on the aisle, totally out of my wheelchair.

I was very mad. Once the show started I forgot all about how mad I was. It was wonderful! We had pretzels and cheese. Emma and I sat next to each other and my parents sat next to her. Straight always comes here around Christmas time.

It was November. I wish Jerome (the only black guy in the group) would have sang Rolling in the Deep. That's my favorite. They even did a song without microphones or speakers, to show people what it is like in rehearsals. It was incredible! They are from Indiana.

A friend of my mom has a daughter-in-law that has a friend, who is in the group. Emma got up to get a t-shirt at intermission. They said the group would be in the lobby after the show if anyone wanted to meet them and get autographs. I really wanted to but, with my chair and being in the crowd, I didn't think it was a good idea. I get to see them this year in November I hope we get good seats again.

We go every year at least once to see a show. I have been there many times to see "Jesus Christ Superstar" and "Wicked." Normally we are in the wheelchair section. Getting to the elevator is always such a challenge. People can be so rude! They don't get out of the way, there are huge line for drinks and especially for the bathrooms. Even so, I love going to the Fox.

Straight No Chaser 2015

Chapter 26

Art Show and Wine Tasting

Angela invited me to an Art show/Wine tasting event. It was on the campus of St. Louis University. All of the art and paintings were done by people who have disabilities. The wine came from a company called 100 Percent. The owner is a father of a child with a disability who is raising money for disability awareness. That's so nice!

The art was very expensive. I think the artists were mostly children. Angela was invited by her friend who is a teacher at SLU. Her name is Professor Myers and she is legally blind. Angela had her Wendy books for sale on a table in the back of the room. She sold two sets of books. Angela let me put my book on the table, too. Not very many people looked at it until I started asking people to towards the end of the night.

We went around to all the exhibits. There was a huge cake on one of the table where the wine was set up. The only thing you had to pay for was a full bottle of wine. Otherwise, they were taking donations for drink by the glass. I'm very glad I went. It was fun. All the people were very nice and we met a lot of people!.

Chapter 27

Babysitting Drake and Sally

I also really enjoy babysitting my niece and nephew, when I am not writing, sewing or crocheting. They are so cute! Drake is 3 and Sally just turned a year old. I have a lot of fun watching them.

Drake is really funny! The things he says sometimes I can't believe came from a three year old. He is also very smart. Drake loves the mall! I think his favorite things are the Train and the Carousal. He also loves to sit and watch "Paw Patrol" all day long though. Sally is really sweet, too. She is learning to say words and crawls around the floor everywhere. Sometimes when my parents and I watch them, we take them places. Sally doesn't usually care what we do. She is very well behaved when we are in public. When she isn't crawling all over she loves to be held. I can't wait until she can talk more. She says a few words now but I mean really talk.

One time Angela and I went to Drake's school to tell the children about Wendy and talk to them, to teach them new things. The kids in his class are so cute! They were absolutely in awe of my wheelchair. I loved showing his teacher my book.

How cute are they?

Chapter 28

Bubble Wrap and Snap Its

I absolutely love running over bubble wrap with my wheelchair so I can hear the popping sound. I put it on the floor or ground and roll in circles over it. For Christmas one year I asked for bubble wrap. My mom and grandma used to get me bubble wrap all the time whenever they came across it. I either pop it with my hands or my chair. It's fun but can really annoy people. Most of the time, I would do it on purpose!

I also love the Fourth of July because sometimes we get Snap It's. Those white things that look like sperm that you throw on the ground. I love throwing them or rolling over them. The Fourth is my favorite holiday, just for those. I look forward to them every year.

There are other parts of summer I like too, barbeques and watermelon. This year my sister and her family came over to celebrate with us a lot. They all went swimming. We had barbeque and on the Fourth, went to see fireworks. Drake even got to help me throw the Snap Its. Dad was not happy that we made a mess and got them all over the drive way. Oops! Dad even found the ones we couldn't pop that went under the van. Hahaha. We all had a great time, except for my dog Nelson, who was afraid of the sounds of the fireworks.

Nelson enjoying the pool and the traditions on the 4th.

Chapter 29

Family Traditions

I also think family traditions are a lot of fun. Every Halloween we used to go to a neighborhood party where my neighbor would dress up like Elvis and give everyone a concert in his garage. He loves Elvis and is really pretty good. During the Thanksgiving and Christmas holidays we have friends and family over, of course, but we also have our local Dierberg's Market prepare and cook the dinner meal.

On my Dad's side we have a family Christmas party and soccer game the week before Christmas every year for as long as I can remember. That's my favorite part of the whole Christmas season. Christmas Eve is a lot of fun, too. The church is decorated so beautifully and then my sister and her family comes over for presents after mass. After we eat and open presents, my Dad goes to my cousin's house in a Santa suit and delivers present to all their grandkids. I love Christmas Eve though it's a bit long. On Christmas day my uncle and his family comes over and we all give him gift cards to give to the poor instead of exchanging presents.

Chapter 30

I am Supergirl!

I have many nicknames but the one I love the most is Supergirl. I love anything that has to do with Superman or Supergirl! I even have a Superman tattoo on my chest in honor of Christopher Reeve and almost got to meet him. I love Christopher Reeve and did an entire research project on him when I was in high school.

I also really like the new series of Supergirl featuring an actress from Glee. It is so full of action! There is a lot about the story of Supergirl and Superman that I didn't know. It's on every Monday night.

I also collect a lot of things with Superman on it. I have gotten many things that have the Superman symbol on them over the years as gifts. I also really love my new Superman sweatshirt my mom bought me. I love super heroes! My sister's third book is about Wendy being a super hero and using her gifts and talents to give back to her community. One of my sister's friends even gave me the nickname The Wheeled American and it stuck. I mostly go by Moochie though.

Chapter 31

Fun and Silly Facts you didn't know about The Wheeled American

My family calls me Mooch because when I was really little, I used to mooch food off of people. I would ask in an adorable way, "Are you going to eat that?" My grandpa thought it was funny when I did that and called me a Mooch. It stuck and to this day, I am either the Mooch or Moochie. Everyone calls me that now.

My absolute favorite color is purple and I used to want everything purple. In high school my favorite teachers would get me gifts that were purple. I was known as princess purple or the purple princess by those teachers. My room in my old house had purple walls with butterfly decals. One of my favorite craft projects was crocheting a dark purple afghan. It turned out so pretty, I kept it for myself. I also made my mom a lavender and royal purple scarf for Mother's day. Oh, the laptop that I am writing this on is purple too. I love all shades of purple.

My favorite animal is a monkey. I used to have a stuffed monkey collection. For a short amount of time I wanted all things monkey as gifts. My grandma still calls me monkey sometimes. When I was younger I wanted to work with monkeys. Angela chose the primate house in Wendy on Wheels goes to the Zoo because at the St. Louis Zoo the primate house is up a really big hill. When we were working to finalize the pictures for her book, we finally got up the hill and there were steps going into the front of the building. I was very disappointed because I really wanted to see the monkeys. We still had fun that day, even though parts of the Zoo are not accessible.

I love butterflies!!! They are my second favorite species. My room is decorated in butterflies and I have clothes and purses with butterflies all over them. I love going to Faust Park to visit the Butterfly House close to where I live! It is a gigantic building where butterflies fly free. Like the Muny, our local outdoor theater, the butterfly house is only open in the summer so it is really hot in there but it's so beautiful! I love going into the gift shop, too. All the items in it have something to do with butterflies. One time my dad came with me and acted like he was slapping them off of him while we were taking a tour around the enclosure. It was really embarrassing and kind of funny at the same time. The best part about sitting in our backyard is seeing butterflies flying around. We have a pool and they seem to be attracted to the cool water.

My favorite things about me are my sense of humor and the fact that I am very driven if there something I want to do. Which kind of goes hand in hand, as I am sitting here writing. I love it when I have an idea that I think is great I can't help but share it! I'm always trying to make everything perfectly written.

In closing, I'd like to thank you for letting me share a little bit about me with you. And giving me the opportunity to help you become a little more aware in the process. I hope you have learned that people with different abilities can do things they just may be in a different way. Thanks so much!! Mandy

Me, at Christmas time, after I lost weight for my surgery.

About the author

Mandy "The Wheeled American" Ruzicka was born in St. Louis. She is a full time wheelchair user due to being born with Spina Bifida. She graduated from Parkway West High School in Chesterfield, MO. She lives at home with her parents and 2 fur babies, Copper and Nelson.

For information on Wendy on Wheels contact Angela Ruzicka at www.wendyonwheels.com

Printed in the United States
By Bookmasters